MENOTTI

ARIAS FOR MEZZO-SOPRANO

8 ARIAS FROM 5 OPERAS

The recording is a collaboration of Hal Leonard and G. Schirmer, Cincinnati Opera, T... ...Conservatory of Music, Cincinnati, and WGUC, Cincinnati, with support from the J. Ralph and Patricia Corbett Foundation.

Evans Mirageas, producer

ED 4385
ISBN 978-1-4234-2752-0

G. SCHIRMER, Inc.

DISTRIBUTED BY

HAL•LEONARD®
CORPORATION
7777 W. BLUEMOUND RD. P.O. BOX 13819 MILWAUKEE, WI 53213

www.schirmer.com
www.halleonard.com

GIAN CARLO MENOTTI
(1911–2007)

Gian Carlo Menotti was born on July 7, 1911, in Cadegliano, Italy. At the age of 7, under the guidance of his mother, he began to compose songs, and four years later he wrote the words and music of his first opera, *The Death of Pierrot*. In 1923 he began his formal musical training at the Verdi Conservatory in Milan. Following the death of his father, his mother took him to the United States, where he was enrolled at Philadelphia's Curtis Institute of Music. There he completed his musical studies, working in composition under Rosario Scalero.

His first mature work, the one-act opera buffa, *Amelia al Ballo*, was premiered in 1937, a success that led to a commission from the National Broadcasting Company to write an opera especially for radio, *The Old Maid and the Thief*, the first such commission ever given. His first ballet, *Sebastian*, followed in 1944, and for this he wrote the scenario as well as the score. After the premiere of his Piano Concerto in 1945, Menotti returned to opera with *The Medium*, shortly joined by *The Telephone*, both enjoying international success.

The Consul, Menotti's first full-length work, won the Pulitzer Prize and the New York Drama Critics Circle award as the best musical play of the year in 1954. By far Menotti's best-known work is the Christmas classic *Amahl and the Night Visitors*, composed for NBC-TV in 1951. This beloved opera celebrated the 50th anniversary of its premiere in 2001, and continues to receive hundreds of performances annually.

Menotti wrote the text to all his operas, the original language being English in every case, with the exception of *Amelia al Ballo*, *The Island God*, and *The Last Savage*, which were first set to Italian words. Recent operas include *The Singing Child* (1993) and *Goya* (1986), written for Plácido Domingo and given its premiere by The Washington Opera. In the summer of 2004 Domingo reprised the role at Vienna's Theater an der Wien. Menotti's most recent vocal works are *Jacob's Prayer* (1997), a commission from the American Choral Directors Association, *Gloria*, written as part of a composite Mass celebrating the 1995 Nobel Peace Prize, *For the Death of Orpheus*, with a premiere by the Atlanta Symphony Orchestra led by Robert Shaw in November 1990, and *Llama de Amor Viva*, premiered in April 1991. A trio for the Verdehr Trio received its world premiere at the Spoleto Festival on Menotti's 85th birthday in July 1996.

In addition to the numerous operatic works, Menotti has enriched the artistic world with ballets, including *Errand into the Maze* (in the repertory of the Martha Graham Dance Company), and *The Unicorn, the Gorgon, and the Manticore*; *Pastorale for Piano and Strings* (1934); *Poemetti*, a suite of piano pieces for children (1937); *The Hero* (1952), a song on a text by Robert Horan; and *Canti della Lontananza*, a cycle of seven songs (1967). He also wrote the librettos to Samuel Barber's operas *Vanessa* and *A Hand of Bridge*.

1958 saw the opening of Menotti's own festival, the Festival of Two Worlds, in Spoleto, Italy. Devoted to the cultural collaboration of Europe and America in a program embracing all the arts, the Spoleto Festival has gone on to be one of the most popular festivals in Europe. The festival literally became "of two worlds" in 1977 with the founding of Spoleto USA in Charleston, South Carolina, which he led until 1993 when he became Director of the Rome Opera. Well into his 90s he continued to direct opera at Spoleto and elsewhere. During the 2005-06 season *The Consul* was produced at Teatro Regio in Italy; performances in the 2004-05 season included productions at the Arizona Opera and in Zurich, Switzerland. Menotti died in Monaco on February 1, 2007, at age 95.

In 1984 Menotti was awarded the Kennedy Center Honor for lifetime achievement in the arts. He was chosen the 1991 "Musician of the Year" by Musical America, inaugurating worldwide tributes to the composer in honor of his 80th birthday. His music has been published by G. Schirmer since 1946.

CONTENTS

Singers on the CD:
Soon Cho (tracks 3, 4, 6)
Liza Forrester (tracks 1, 2, 5)
Elizabeth Pojanowski (track 7)
Kathleen Sonnentag (track 8)

Pianists:
Mark Gibson (tracks 3, 4, 6, 7)
Carol Walker (tracks 1, 2, 5)
Richard Walters (track 8)

NOTES ON THE ARIAS

THE MEDIUM
• music and libretto by Gian Carlo Menotti
• first performed on May 8, 1946 at Columbia University, New York City; opened on Broadway (on a double bill with The Telephone) on May 1, 1947 at the Ethel Barrymore Theater, New York City

Afraid, am I afraid?

(Baba's Aria)

from Act II
setting: the outskirts of a great city, the present; Madame Flora's parlor
character: Baba
Baba, or Madame Flora, is a phony medium who stages seances for money. She is convinced that a ghostly hand clutched at her throat during a seance, and is terrified. She drinks herself into a stupor before this mad scene.

THE CONSUL
• music and libretto by Gian Carlo Menotti
• first performed on March 1, 1950 at the Schubert Theater in Philadelphia; opened on Broadway on March 15, 1950 at the Ethel Barrymore Theatre, New York City

Shall we ever see the end of all this!

from Act I, scene 1
setting: a European police state, the present; the apartment of John and Madga Sorel
character: the Mother

A family struggles against the tyranny of a police state with tragic consequences in this cold war melodrama. Freedom activist John Sorel has been going to secret meetings. He has returned home wounded by the police, and is quickly hidden as they approach the apartment. As the secret police agents make their intrusive search, John's mother (called the Mother in the opera), who also lives in the apartment, sings this lament.

Lullaby

from Act II, scene 1
setting: a European police state, the present; the apartment of John and Madga Sorel
character: the Mother

John's mother tries tickling her sickly grandchild, making faces and funny sounds to make him smile and laugh, but the child is unresponsive. She peers into the cradle and sings a concerned lullaby.

The Empty-handed Traveler

from Act II, scene 1
setting: a European police state, the present; the apartment of John and Madga Sorel
character: the Mother

Magda and John Sorel's baby boy has died. His grandmother (called the Mother) weeps at the cradleside upon discovering his body. Magda replies "Oh, no! Not that! It is too soon to cry. He may still hear us…sh, Mother, sh!" The aria then begins. The two women mourn together as the curtain falls on the scene.

The material in this section was previously published in the *G. Schirmer American Aria Anthology*, edited by Richard Walters.

Oh, those faces!

from Act III, scene 1
setting: a European police state, the present; the office of the Consul of a neighboring country
character: the Secretary

The secretary at the consulate has spent another long day of listening to exit visa requests. Preparing to leave, she turns out all the lights except the lamp on her desk, and is startled and haunted by visions of the many desperate people who have passed through her office.

AMAHL AND THE NIGHT VISITORS
• music and libretto by Gian Carlo Menotti
• commissioned by NBC Television; first performed in a live broadcast on December 24, 1951

All that gold!

in one act
setting: the Italian hills at the time of the birth of Christ; a poor woman's home and yard
character: Amahl's Mother

This Christmas opera tells the story of a crippled boy who is miraculously healed when he offers his crutch as a gift to the newborn Christ. The three Magi spend the night at a poor widow's home, on their journey to take gifts to the baby Jesus. Amahl's mother is sleepless, thinking about the gold the visitors carry and her son's impoverished predicament. The aria ends as the Page awakens and alerts the kings as she is stealing the treasure. The role of the Mother may be sung either by a soprano or mezzo-soprano. Her aria is more vocally suitable for a mezzo-soprano as a stand-alone solo.

THE SAINT OF BLEECKER STREET
• music and libretto by Gian Carlo Menotti
• opened on Broadway on December 27, 1954 at the Broadway Theatre, New York City

Ah, Michele, don't you know

from: Act II
setting: Greenwich Village, New York City, the present; outside an Italian restaurant where a wedding reception is taking place
character: Desideria

Michele and Annina, brother and sister, are both driven by Catholicism, she by her deep faith and the stigmata that appear on her hands, he by hatred of religion. Michele and his girlfriend Desideria stand outside a Greenwich Village restaurant arguing. The conservative Catholic neighbors at the wedding shun her because of her unmarried relationship with Michele. Desideria is frustrated at Michele's extreme protection of his sister. Forcing him to prove he's not ashamed of her, Desideria asks if he will take her with him into the wedding reception. When he does not reply, she sings the aria.

THE HERO

- music and libretto by Gian Carlo Menotti
- commissioned by the Opera Company of Philadelphia in recognition of the nation's bicentennial; first performed on June 1, 1976 at the Academy of Music, Philadelphia

Look at all those things

from: Act I
setting: United States, the present day; an apartment
character: Mildred

The opera is a soft-edged satire of an American who unwittingly falls victim to political fraud, conceived in the spirit of the times following Watergate. David has been sleeping for ten years, which has made him a celebrity, thanks to the exploitation of the situation by his opportunistic wife, Mildred. Their home has become a lucrative tourist attraction. Mildred is getting ready for tomorrow's unveiling ceremony of a monument to the sleeping "hero," who has greatly enhanced the local economy. The village shopkeepers arrive to deliver gifts to her for the occasion. She sees them out and bursts into gleeful laughter at her good fortune, singing to her cousin Barbara, who works with Mildred giving tours and selling tickets. David later awakens. There is an attempted cover-up to retain the tourism business, but a truthful hero ultimately prevails.

MENOTTI

ARIAS FOR MEZZO-SOPRANO

Afraid, am I afraid?

(Baba's Aria)

from

THE MEDIUM

Gian Carlo Menotti

ter - ri - ble things! Wo - men scream - ing as they were mur - dered, and men's hands drip - ping with blood, and men haunt - ed by knives. And lit - tle gro - tesque chil - dren drained white _____ by the vo - ra - cious - ness of filth, and loath - some old men in - sane with vice, and young men with

What un - seen ghost stands by my side? No, no, it can - not be the

dead! The dead... the dead... the

Andante molto maestoso ♩ = 52

dead nev - er come back. They sink down in the dust with

accelerando molto   *allarg. molto*

no eyes to dream and no si - lence to keep, no se - crets to hide!

Lentissimo

(drowsily and a little drunkenly)

poco rall.

Gone, emp - ty, noth-ing, noth-ing.

Largamente ♪ = 56

(Wheeling about in her chair, she breaks off the song with a startled cry.)

"O black swan, where, oh, where ____ is my lov - er gone?"

(Her voice shaking, scarcely daring to breathe, she stares fixedly into the darkness and listens.)

(turning again with a cry)

(shouted) *lunga*

*Who's there? "O black swan, O black swan..."

(shouted) *lunga*

(After a long silence, with a sigh of relief)

What? Noth - ing, but then if there is

*No breath should be taken between the last note and the spoken phrase.

(Her laughter has now reached an hysterical pitch.)

(She suddenly stops laughing)

O

Tempo I°

God, for - give my sins, I'm sick and old,

poco rall.

for - give my sins, I'm sick and old.

Shall we ever see the end of all this!

from
THE CONSUL

Gian Carlo Menotti

we have seen too much be - tray - al.

We can no long-er keep our si - lence!

E - ven death _____ seems too slow _____

_____ in grant-ing us our rest.

Lullaby
from
THE CONSUL

Gian Carlo Menotti

The Empty-handed Traveler

from
THE CONSUL

Gian Carlo Menotti

I shall nev-er see a-gain; for John, my son, whom I must

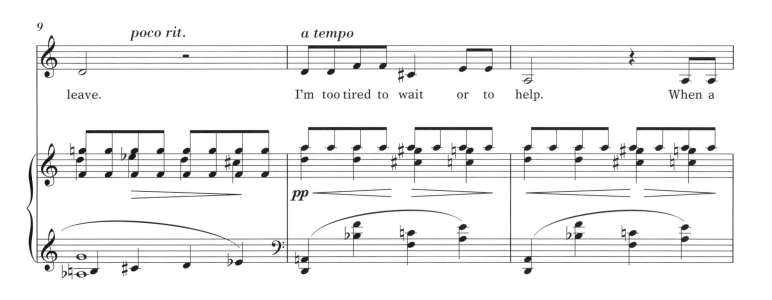

poco rit. a tempo

leave. I'm too tired to wait or to help. When a

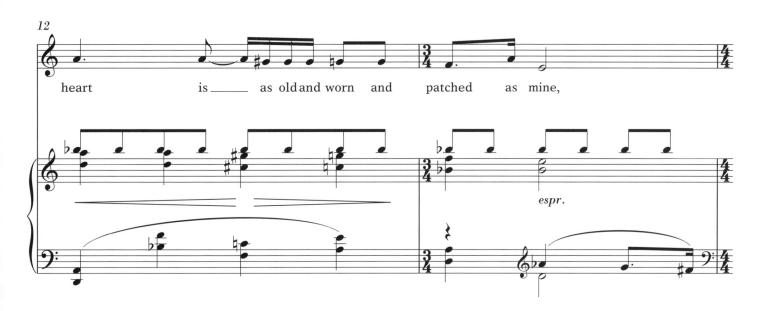

heart is _____ as old and worn and patched as mine,

espr.

Less - er things can break it than the death - sigh of a child.

poco movendo ma senza correre

Old peo - ple live for sim - ple things: to see a birth, to

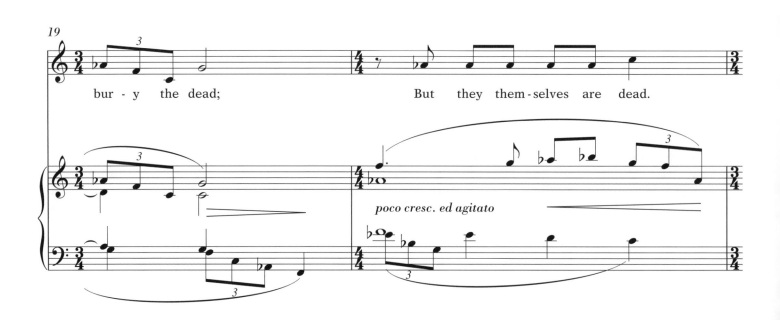

bur - y the dead; But they them - selves are dead.

poco cresc. ed agitato

They live on bor-rowed breath, and once the thing is done, they quick - ly crum - ble in - to dust.

Now let me fold my things

and lock my doors. I leave be - hind me

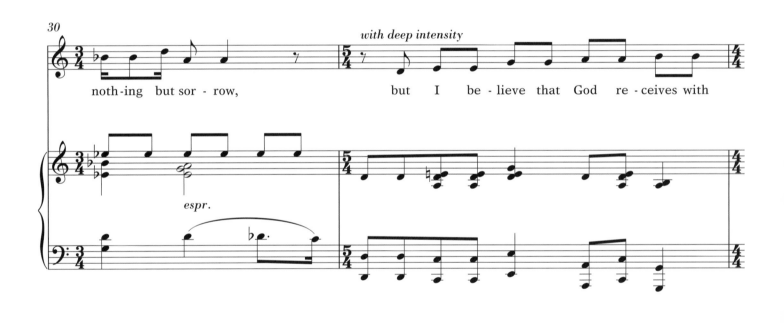

noth - ing but sor - row, but I be - lieve that God re - ceives with

kind - ness the emp - ty - hand - ed trav - el - er.

Oh, those faces!

from
THE CONSUL

Gian Carlo Menotti

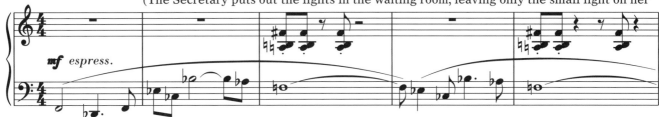

bone - less, pale _____ in the dust - y

sun.

One must try not to re-mem - ber. One ___ must not think.

(She stumbles back to her desk, only to be confronted by the lists of names.)

Oth-er-wise, _ how can one do an-y work? Ah, _____ those names!_ All ___ those names!_

All that gold!
from
AMAHL AND THE NIGHT VISITORS

Gian Carlo Menotti

Ah, Michele, don't you know

from
THE SAINT OF BLEECKER STREET

Gian Carlo Menotti

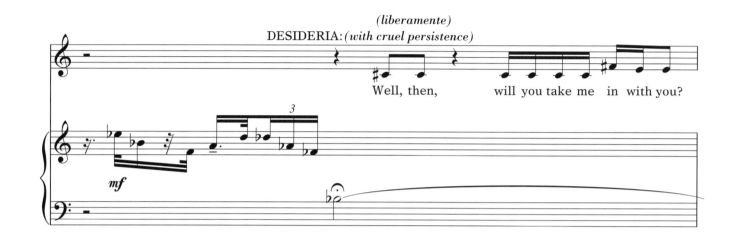

hate at the sound of one word, if the word is said too late?

Love can nev - er heal its wounds un - less the cry is

an - swered, un - less the scar is seen.

Poco più mosso

All the tears one weeps a - lone do

poco rit.   *a tempo*

not un - lock the pound-ing gates of the heart. Like

stars they fall in death - ly still - ness

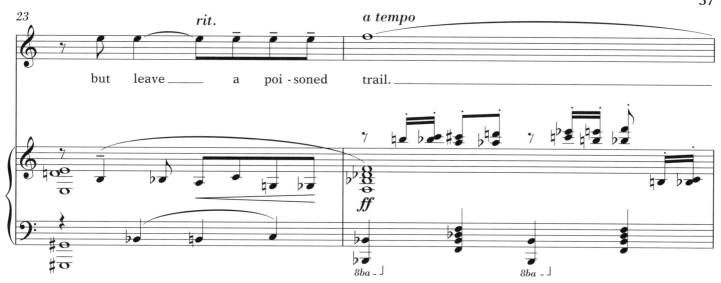

but leave ___ a poi - soned trail. ___

On - ly he, ___ whose

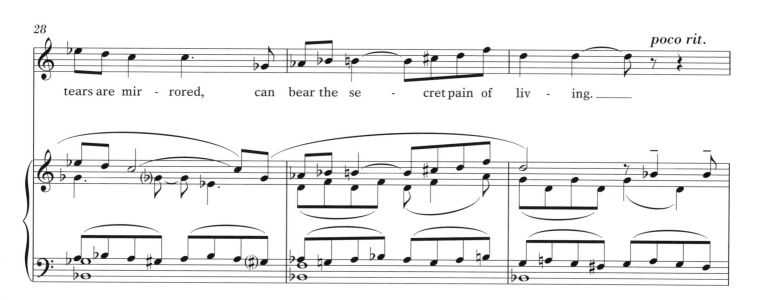

tears are mir - rored, can bear the se - cret pain of liv - ing. ___

Those of us, ___ who find our love on earth, ___ must cel - e - brate ___ our fleet-ing

tri - umph. Who wel - comes love in

si - lence or hides it like a crime,

shall soon run to the waste - lands to es-cape its blind - ing

ven - geance.

Tempo I

Ah, _____ Mi -che - le,

don't for - get   that   love   is   a

pit - i - less hunt - er___ when   al - lied   with

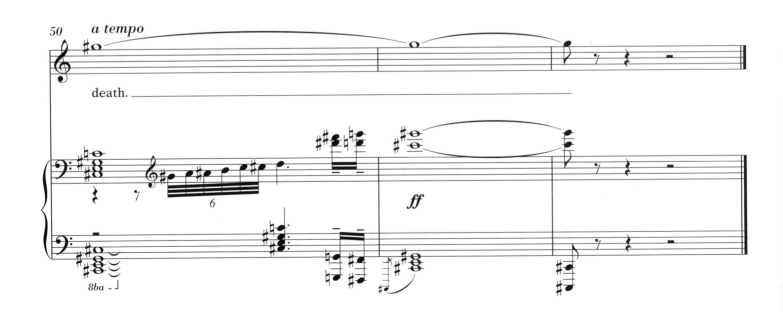

death. ___

Look at all those things

from
THE HERO

Gian Carlo Menotti

The small sized notes may be omitted if necessary in this difficult piano reduction.

neck - lace, look at this ring. All so much more ex -

pen - sive than an - y - thing I or - dered, joy, _____

joy, _____ I'm so ex - cit - ed! So ver - y, ver - y

hap - py. But why do you look so sad? Feel - ing _____

liberamente   *teasingly*

colla voce

35 next to a dull man. On-ly a few of us can cap-ture a

40 man like mine and lead a life of bliss, with all the é-lite and mon-ey-

45 *poco rall.* *a tempo* peo-ple at one's feet. But one must be pret - ty, have plen-ty of

50 *poco rall.* *a tempo* flair and sa-voir - faire, _____ Know how to be reck - less,

I can fire, in - spire, _____ I was not meant to

mar - ry Tom, Dick and Har - ry be-cause I'm pret - ty,

I have good style and a good smile, _____

Men can - not re - sist me when asked to as -

Lyrics:

sist me. How can wom-en help it but de-test me?

I was born to be a star,

to be en - vied, to be a - dored.

But it is get - ting late

and I must try my clothes on. Some-one might call _____

to say hel - lo, _____ Ah, _____

— ah, _____ I shall slay them

all. _____